LATEST EDITION

GEN Z

DICTIONARY

MAYNARD GILDON

Gen Z Dictionary

Mastering the Modern Language of Gen Z With a Fun and Entertaining Guide to Slang, Expressions, and Culture

Maynard Gildon

COPYRIGHTS

CONTENTS

Letter to Readers..9

Introduction:..1

A... 6

B...13

C...21

D... 28

E... 36

F... 42

G... 49

H... 56

I... 62

J... 68

K... 74

L... 80

M... 86

N... 92

O... 98

P... 103

Q... 109

R... 114

S... 119

T...124
U...129
V...134
W..139
X...144
Y...147
Z...151
Fun Extras...155

Letter to Readers

Dear Reader,

Welcome to the lively and colorful world of *Gen Z Dictionary*! This book is your ultimate guide to mastering the language, expressions, and culture that define Generation Z. Whether you're a curious parent, a teacher trying to keep up, or a fellow Zoomer looking to deepen your slang game, this book was created with you in mind.

Language is more than just words—it's a reflection of identity, culture, and connection. Gen Z has taken this to heart, crafting a dynamic vocabulary that's as innovative and creative as the generation itself. From TikTok trends to gaming jargon, these terms are more than slang; they're windows into how Gen Z sees the world, expresses themselves, and builds community.

This book is designed to be fun, engaging, and informative. You'll laugh, learn, and maybe even find a new favorite phrase to sprinkle into your own conversations. But most importantly, it's a celebration of how language evolves to capture the spirit of its time.

As you flip through the pages, I hope you'll approach this dictionary with curiosity and an open mind. Dive into the humor, embrace the absurdity, and appreciate the creativity that makes Gen Z's language so unique. Who knows? You might even find yourself saying "slay" or "yeet" without a second thought by the end of it!

Thank you for picking up this book and joining me on this linguistic journey. Let's celebrate the innovation, wit, and sheer audacity of Gen Z—one phrase at a time.

Yass Queen and happy reading,

[Maynard Gildon]

Introduction:

A Crash Course in Gen Z Speak

Why Learn Gen Z Lingo?

Imagine walking into a room where everyone's speaking a language that sounds familiar but somehow feels like an entirely different dialect. You catch snippets: "No cap," "That's a whole mood," "It's giving main character energy." You nod along, pretending to understand, but deep down, you feel a little... lost. Welcome to the world of Gen Z lingo, a vibrant and ever-evolving tapestry of words and phrases that reflect the spirit of a generation unlike any other.

Gen Z's language isn't just about trendy slang—it's a window into their worldview. Each term, meme, or viral phrase carries the weight of cultural nuances, inside jokes, and a digital-first mindset. Learning this lingo isn't about "keeping up with the kids." It's about bridging generational gaps, understanding the humor and priorities of a group redefining communication, and, let's face it, staying relevant in a world where emojis sometimes speak louder than words.

Language has always been a tool of connection. Just as Shakespeare crafted his sonnets to reflect the ethos of his era, Gen Z uses language to embody theirs. Learning their lingo means more than decoding memes; it's about embracing a new way to connect with humor, empathy, and cultural savvy.

How Language Shapes Culture

Gen Z doesn't just talk—they vibe. Their communication style is infused with emotion, aesthetic, and a deep understanding of cultural context. It's not uncommon for a single word or phrase to encapsulate an entire narrative. Take "vibe check," for instance: it's not just about gauging the atmosphere, but about sensing alignment, energy, and authenticity in a moment.

This generation has grown up with social media as a second language, and their vocabulary reflects this digital fluency. Memes, TikTok trends, and Twitter threads have become modern-day forums where language is born, tested, and immortalized. A single viral phrase can ripple across platforms, transforming from a niche joke to a global phenomenon in days. Remember when "sheesh" became a universal exclamation of approval, complete with the finger-pointing meme? That's the power of Gen Z culture at work.

Language, for Gen Z, isn't static. It's a living, breathing organism that evolves with every trending hashtag, meme format, or cultural shift. Words are repurposed ("fire" for amazing), phrases are given new life ("that's on periodt"), and entire conversations are boiled down into emojis and abbreviations. The result is a linguistic landscape that's dynamic, playful, and deeply reflective of the digital age.

What Makes Gen Z Unique?

To understand Gen Z lingo, you first need to understand Gen Z. Born roughly between 1997 and 2012, this generation has grown up in a world shaped by rapid technological advancement, social justice movements, and a global pandemic. They're digital natives, but they're also deeply introspective, socially conscious, and unafraid to challenge norms.

Gen Z's language is a reflection of their unique experiences. Words like "ghosting" and "situationship" capture the complexities of modern relationships in a hyperconnected world. Phrases like "sending it" and "main character energy" reflect their YOLO (You Only Live Once) approach to life, where seizing the moment is paramount. And then there's their humor—dry, ironic, and often self-deprecating—best exemplified by phrases like "dead" to express uncontrollable laughter.

What sets Gen Z apart is their ability to merge the personal with the universal. Their language is deeply rooted in individual expression, yet it's designed to resonate with millions. This paradox—deeply personal yet inherently communal—is the hallmark of Gen Z communication.

How to Use This Dictionary

This dictionary is your ultimate guide to understanding, interpreting, and maybe even adopting Gen Z lingo. But before you dive in, here are a few tips to get the most out of it:

1. **Context is Key**: Many Gen Z terms can mean different things depending on how they're used. For example, "mood" can refer to something relatable, but "big mood" amplifies that relatability into a universal truth. Pay attention to the examples provided to grasp the nuances.
2. **Don't Overthink It**: Gen Z language is often playful and lighthearted. If a phrase like "It's giving..." confuses you, just remember it's about

describing a vibe or essence. Don't get bogged down in literal meanings.

3. **Be Open to Experimentation**: Language is meant to be fun! Try slipping a term or two into your conversations. Whether you're describing your "drip" (fashion) or acknowledging a "W" (win), embrace the playfulness.

4. **Evolve with It**: Gen Z lingo is constantly changing. This dictionary provides a snapshot of the most popular terms and phrases, but new ones will emerge. Think of this as your foundation for staying curious and adaptable.

5. **Enjoy the Journey**: Learning Gen Z lingo isn't about perfecting it; it's about engaging with a new way of seeing the world. Whether you're an adult trying to decode your kids' texts or a Gen Z-er looking to connect with peers, have fun with it!

A

The Beginning of the Alphabet and All the Vibes

Language is where it all starts, and in the Gen Z universe, "A" isn't just the first letter—it's the beginning of a world filled with aesthetics, algorithms, and a dash of attitude. Let's dive into the most iconic and entertaining terms starting with "A." Get ready to level up your lingo.

Aesthetic

Definition: A specific vibe, style, or look, often tied to visual themes or personal expression. Gen Z's obsession with aesthetics reflects their knack for curating their lives down to the tiniest detail—whether it's their Instagram feed, outfit, or Spotify playlist.

Example: "Her whole aesthetic is cottagecore with those floral dresses and vintage tea sets."

Cultural Note: Popular aesthetics include cottagecore (whimsical countryside vibes), dark academia (moody intellectual vibes), and Y2K (early 2000s throwbacks). Bonus points if your aesthetic has its own TikTok niche.

Algorithm

Definition: The mysterious and all-powerful digital force curating what you see on social media. For Gen Z, understanding the algorithm is like understanding the laws of gravity—it's a foundational part of navigating their digital lives.

Example: "The algorithm must know I'm obsessed with dog videos because that's all I see on my FYP."

Pro Tip: Want to beat the algorithm? Engage, comment, and "like" your favorite content. Just don't complain too loudly about the algorithm; it might actually retaliate (kidding… or not).

Alt

Definition: Short for "alternative," this term describes a subculture or aesthetic that's edgy, unconventional, or outside the mainstream. Think piercings, thrifted clothes, and listening to indie bands no one's heard of yet.

Example: "I'm not a regular teenager; I'm alt."

Cultural Note: The "alt" aesthetic has its roots in punk and emo subcultures but has evolved into a broader term for anyone embracing individuality over mainstream trends.

And I Oop

Definition: A viral phrase used to express surprise, shock, or when you've made a mistake and don't know what to say. Originally coined by drag queen Jasmine Masters, it quickly became a cultural phenomenon.

Example: "I dropped my phone in the toilet, and I oop."

Cultural Note: This phrase is often paired with exaggerated hand gestures and dramatic facial expressions for comedic effect. It's peak Gen Z humor—random, relatable, and ridiculously over-the-top.

ASMR (Autonomous Sensory Meridian Response)

Definition: A tingling sensation that runs down your spine triggered by specific sounds or visuals. It's also a massive trend on YouTube and TikTok, where creators whisper, tap, or crunch objects to give viewers that satisfying "tingle."

Example: "I watch ASMR videos every night to help me fall asleep."

Cultural Note: Whether you love it or find it super weird, ASMR has become a Gen Z-approved relaxation tool. Just don't judge the person in your life who's addicted to "soap cutting" videos—they're vibing.

Ask

Definition: A subtle but powerful shift in how Gen Z uses this word. It's no longer just a verb; it's now a noun, often used in professional or casual contexts to describe a request.

Example: "That's a big ask, but I'll see what I can do."

Pro Tip: Using "ask" this way might make you sound super in-the-know. Just remember—it's not the same as a demand.

Anti-Hero

Definition: A character (or person) who embraces their flaws and doesn't pretend to be perfect. Thanks to Taylor Swift's hit song "Anti-Hero," the term has been catapulted back into mainstream pop culture.

Example: "It's me, hi, I'm the anti-hero."

Cultural Note: Gen Z loves an anti-hero because they're relatable, messy, and unapologetically human. Perfect is boring, anyway.

Awks

Definition: A shortened version of "awkward," used to describe an uncomfortable or embarrassing situation. Bonus points for pairing it with a dramatic pause.

Example: "I accidentally liked their Instagram post from 2016. Awks."

Pro Tip: If you ever feel the urge to say "awks," lean into it. The word is awkwardly charming, just like the moments it describes.

Authentic

Definition: Being genuine, real, or true to oneself. Gen Z prizes authenticity above all else in a world often dominated by filters and curated personas.

Example: "Her content is so authentic—she's not trying to be someone she's not."

Cultural Note: The rise of "authenticity" reflects a pushback against the perfectionism of earlier social media eras. It's not about being flawless; it's about being real, flaws and all.

AF

Definition: Short for "as f***," used to emphasize something intensely or extremely.

Example: "I'm tired AF after that long day."

Cultural Note: While casual, this phrase is wildly popular in informal settings. Just maybe avoid using it at a family dinner.

Avatar

Definition: A digital representation of yourself, often used in gaming, virtual reality, or social media platforms.

Example: "I customized my avatar to look just like me, but cooler."

Cultural Note: Avatars have become more significant as virtual spaces like the metaverse gain traction, letting people express themselves in creative ways.

B

Bringing the Buzz and the Bussin'

Gen Z's love for language innovation doesn't stop at "A"—"B" is where things really start to pop. From clever phrases to cultural buzzwords, "B" brings a blend of attitude, humor, and modern-day wisdom. Let's jump into this section and explore the bold, the brilliant, and the downright "bussin'" language that makes Gen Z speak so captivating.

Bet

Definition: A term used to confirm, agree, or express approval. Think of it as Gen Z's cooler, shorter equivalent of "Okay" or "I'm down."

Example: "You coming to the party tonight?" "Bet."

Cultural Note: Short, snappy, and versatile, "Bet" reflects Gen Z's preference for minimalism in communication. Bonus points for using it to hype up plans.

Bussin'

Definition: A term used to describe something that's exceptionally good, especially food.

Example: "These tacos are bussin', no cap!"

Cultural Note: Originating in AAVE (African American Vernacular English), "bussin'" has become a staple of Gen Z slang. Whether it's a home-cooked meal or a viral TikTok recipe, if it's "bussin'," it's worth savoring.

Big Mood

Definition: An exaggerated way of saying "I can relate" or "Same." Used when something encapsulates your current vibe or emotion perfectly.

Example: "That meme of the dog wrapped in a blanket? Big mood."

Cultural Note: Like its simpler cousin "Mood," "Big Mood" leans into Gen Z's love for hyper-relatability and expressive shorthand.

Bread

Definition: Money or financial success. Sometimes used as "getting the bread" to mean earning income or achieving financial goals.

Example: "I'm grinding hard to get this bread."

Pro Tip: Pair it with hustle-related terms for ultimate Gen Z flair, like "securing the bag" (another money-related phrase).

Blessed

Definition: Feeling grateful, fortunate, or lucky. Often used sincerely but can also be ironic.

Example: "Woke up today with my iced coffee ready. Feeling blessed."

Cultural Note: Pair it with hashtags like #grateful or #blessed for a post-modern take on showing appreciation.

Boujee

Definition: Short for "bourgeoisie," it describes someone (or something) fancy, high-end, or luxurious.

Example: "We're going boujee tonight—reservation at the rooftop restaurant."

Cultural Note: Often paired with humor to describe people or situations that might be "over-the-top" or extra in their pursuit of sophistication.

Based

Definition: Being unapologetically yourself or having an opinion that's not influenced by others.

Example: "She's so based for calling out those fake friends."

Cultural Note: Originally popularized in online communities, "based" has evolved into a broader term of praise for authenticity and courage.

Boomer

Definition: A term originally referring to Baby Boomers but now used (often humorously or sarcastically) to describe anyone who seems out of touch or resistant to modern trends.

Example: "He asked how to save a TikTok—total boomer move."

Cultural Note: Gen Z's use of "boomer" is less about age and more about attitude. If you're stuck in the past, you might just get labeled one.

Bop

Definition: A song that's undeniably catchy and fun to listen to.

Example: "This new track by Dua Lipa? Total bop."

Pro Tip: If a song makes you want to hit repeat, call it a bop and watch the nods of approval roll in.

Baddie

Definition: Someone who's confident, stylish, and unapologetically themselves. Often used to describe a strong, independent person with a killer sense of fashion.

Example: "She walked in like a total baddie in that red dress."

Cultural Note: The term is often associated with Instagram influencers or TikTok stars who exude confidence and charm.

BRB (Be Right Back)

Definition: An abbreviation used in text or online chats to let someone know you'll be away momentarily.

Example: "Gotta grab a snack, BRB."

Cultural Note: While "BRB" originates from early internet slang, it's still widely used today. It's a nod to Gen Z's blend of retro and modern communication styles.

Bye Felicia

Definition: A dismissive phrase used to tell someone they're irrelevant or not worth engaging with. Originated from the 1995 movie *Friday* and later popularized by memes.

Example: "You're still mad about that? Bye Felicia."

Cultural Note: Perfect for dramatic exits or shutting down unnecessary drama with a touch of humor.

Brain Rot

Definition: The feeling of being overly consumed by something, usually in an ironic or self-aware way.

Example: "I've watched this show five times already. Absolute brain rot."

Cultural Note: Often used to describe obsessive binge-watching, gaming, or scrolling through TikTok.

Boss

Definition: A term of respect for someone who's in charge, confident, or making moves.

Example: "She handled that presentation like a boss."

Cultural Note: Can be used ironically or sincerely, depending on context. Either way, it's a power move.

Blame It on the Algorithm

Definition: A phrase used to jokingly or seriously attribute something unexpected to social media algorithms.

Example: "I ended up on conspiracy theory TikTok. Blame it on the algorithm."

Cultural Note: Highlights Gen Z's awareness of how digital platforms influence their experiences and interests.

C

Gen Z's knack for redefining language shines brightly in the letter "C." Whether it's clever cultural commentary, comedic expressions, or cutting-edge slang, "C" brings both depth and hilarity to their lexicon. Let's explore the captivating world of "C," where phrases like "Cancel Culture" and "Clout" make waves.

Cancel Culture

Definition: A phenomenon where public figures or entities are boycotted or held accountable for problematic actions or statements, often amplified by social media.

Example: "That influencer got canceled after those tweets resurfaced."

Cultural Note: While "canceling" often sparks heated debates about accountability versus mob mentality, it remains a powerful tool for highlighting injustice. Gen Z uses it to call out bad behavior but also to poke fun at overreactions.

Clout

Definition: Influence, fame, or popularity, particularly on social media. Often pursued for validation or as a status symbol.

Example: "She's only hanging out with him for the clout."

Cultural Note: Chasing clout can be seen as either savvy or shallow, depending on the context. Bonus: Pair it with "Clout Chaser" to describe someone overly eager for attention.

Cap

Definition: A lie or falsehood. Often used in phrases like "No Cap" to mean "No lie" or "I'm being honest."

Example: "That's cap. You did not meet Harry Styles."

Cultural Note: Short, punchy, and direct, "Cap" reflects Gen Z's love for minimalistic yet impactful slang.

Cringe

Definition: Something so awkward, embarrassing, or out-of-touch that it makes you physically recoil.
Example: "That attempt to dance on TikTok was pure cringe."
Cultural Note: Gen Z thrives on irony, so "cringe" isn't always negative—it can also be endearing when done with self-awareness.

Catfish

Definition: Pretending to be someone you're not online, often using fake photos or profiles.
Example: "I thought I was talking to a model, but I got catfished."
Pro Tip: Trust your instincts and reverse-search those profile pictures!

CEO of...

Definition: A humorous way of saying someone excels at something or embodies a particular trait.
Example: "She's the CEO of procrastination."

Cultural Note: This phrase adds playful exaggeration to everyday observations and is a prime example of Gen Z's love for turning serious concepts into jokes.

Chill

Definition: Relaxed, easy-going, or free from drama. Can also mean to hang out casually.
Example: "We're just chilling at my place tonight."
Cultural Note: Being "chill" is the ultimate compliment in Gen Z culture. The phrase is a personality goal as much as it is a state of being.

Caught in 4K

Definition: Getting exposed or caught red-handed, often with undeniable proof (like a high-definition video).
Example: "He said he wasn't at the party, but we caught him in 4K."
Cultural Note: This phrase highlights Gen Z's tech-savvy nature and their love for calling out inconsistencies with receipts.

Clown

Definition: Someone who acts foolishly, especially in romantic situations. Can also refer to oneself in a moment of regret or poor judgment.
Example: "I waited three hours for his reply. Guess I'm the clown."
Cultural Note: Often accompanied by the clown emoji (🤡), this term captures the self-deprecating humor Gen Z is known for.

Crying in the Club

Definition: A dramatic way to describe feeling emotional or overwhelmed, often ironically.
Example: "That scene in the movie had me crying in the club."
Pro Tip: Use this phrase even if you're nowhere near a club. It's all about the dramatic flair.

Clean

Definition: Something impressive, sleek, or visually appealing.

Example: "That outfit is so clean."

Cultural Note: Can apply to anything from fashion to art, reflecting Gen Z's appreciation for minimalism and aesthetics.

Catch These Hands

Definition: A humorous or semi-serious way of saying someone is ready to fight.

Example: "You took the last slice of pizza? Catch these hands."

Cultural Note: Often used playfully rather than as an actual threat, highlighting Gen Z's ability to turn confrontation into comedy.

Cursed

Definition: Something so bizarre, unsettling, or chaotic that it feels supernaturally wrong.

Example: "This video of a dog walking on two legs is cursed."

Cultural Note: "Cursed" content is a staple of Gen Z humor, thriving on the absurd and the unexpected.

D

Dead, Drip, and the Depths of Gen Z Humor

The letter "D" in Gen Z lingo packs a punch, with terms that are equal parts hilarious, iconic, and deeply relatable. Whether it's describing an emotional state ("Dead"), appreciating someone's fashion sense ("Drip"), or diving into dry humor, "D" takes center stage with style and substance. Let's decode the delightful world of "D."

Dead

Definition: A hyperbolic expression used to convey that something is so funny it's metaphorically "killed" you with laughter. Often paired with emojis like the skull (💀) for dramatic effect.

Example: "That meme had me dead!"

Cultural Note: For a generation that thrives on exaggerated humor, "Dead" is the ultimate badge of comedic approval.

Drip

Definition: Refers to stylish clothing, accessories, or an overall fashionable appearance. It's all about having a sleek, confident vibe.

Example: "Check out his drip—those sneakers are fire!"

Cultural Note: The term "Drip" has roots in hip-hop culture and has been embraced by Gen Z as the go-to word for describing standout style.

Doing the Most

Definition: Acting overly dramatic, extra, or trying too hard to impress.

Example: "She showed up in a ball gown to a casual dinner. She's doing the most."

Cultural Note: Gen Z uses this phrase to gently (or not-so-gently) call out over-the-top behavior while keeping it lighthearted.

Dry Texting

Definition: Sending short, unenthusiastic, or non-engaging messages in a conversation.

Example: "I'm trying to make plans, but he's so dry texting me. It's all 'k' and 'cool.'"

Cultural Note: Dry texting is a universal pet peeve for Gen Z, who value meaningful digital interactions as much as face-to-face ones.

Deadass

Definition: A serious or straightforward way of saying "I'm being completely honest" or "for real."

Example: "You're really wearing Crocs to prom? Deadass?"

Cultural Note: This term blends humor with sincerity, making it a staple for expressing disbelief or conviction.

Down Bad

Definition: A humorous way to describe someone who's desperate, especially in romantic or emotional situations.

Example: "He texted her 'Good morning' three days in a row with no reply. He's down bad."

Cultural Note: While it's often used teasingly, "Down

Bad" also highlights the universal struggle of unrequited feelings.

Default Setting

Definition: Describes someone's plain or unremarkable behavior, style, or attitude. Think of it as calling someone a blank slate.
Example: "He's nice, but his outfit is giving default settings."
Pro Tip: Use this phrase sparingly—it's a humorous jab but can sting if not delivered playfully.

Dank

Definition: Originally a term for high-quality marijuana, it has evolved to describe memes or content that are absurd, edgy, or ridiculously funny.
Example: "That meme about time zones? Pure dank humor."
Cultural Note: Dank humor often walks the line between clever and chaotic, making it a favorite among Gen Z internet circles.

Dragged

Definition: To criticize or roast someone, often in a public or exaggerated way.

Example: "He got dragged on Twitter for that outdated opinion."

Cultural Note: Dragging can range from light-hearted teasing to full-blown internet takedowns, depending on the severity of the offense.

Digital Footprint

Definition: The trail of information someone leaves online, including posts, comments, and personal data.

Example: "Be careful what you post; your digital footprint lasts forever."

Cultural Note: As digital natives, Gen Z is hyper-aware of how their online presence impacts their reputation and future opportunities.

Don't Trip

Definition: A phrase used to reassure someone or tell them not to worry.
Example: "We're running late, but don't trip—the movie hasn't started yet."
Cultural Note: This chill, calming phrase embodies the Gen Z ethos of going with the flow.

Doomscrolling

Definition: The act of obsessively scrolling through negative news or upsetting content, often late at night.
Example: "I stayed up doomscrolling about climate change and couldn't sleep."
Cultural Note: While Gen Z is known for being informed and engaged, they also recognize the mental toll of consuming too much bad news.

Done Up

Definition: Refers to someone being dressed up or glammed out for an occasion.
Example: "She got done up for that wedding—hair, nails, everything on point."

Cultural Note: Getting "done up" is a celebration of effort and style, often shared proudly on social media.

DMs (Direct Messages)

Definition: Private messages sent on social media platforms like Instagram or Twitter. Often used as a way to flirt or communicate discreetly.
Example: "He slid into my DMs with a corny pick-up line."
Cultural Note: DMs are both a digital space for casual connections and the birthplace of countless internet romances.

Double Text

Definition: Sending a second message before the recipient has replied to the first, often seen as a bold or desperate move.
Example: "I double-texted him because I couldn't wait for his reply."
Cultural Note: Double texting is a calculated risk—it can show eagerness or come across as overbearing, depending on the context.

Deets

Definition: Short for "details," often used when asking for or sharing information.

Example: "Send me the deets for the party tonight."

Cultural Note: Casual and efficient, "Deets" aligns perfectly with Gen Z's preference for abbreviations and quick communication.

E

Extra, Emo, and Everything in Between

The letter "E" in Gen Z lingo brings an electrifying mix of dramatic flair, self-expression, and internet culture. From describing over-the-top behavior ("Extra") to exploring niche aesthetics ("E-girl/E-boy"), the "E" section dives into the expressive and entertaining facets of Gen Z's language. Let's explore the essentials of "E" and unlock its exuberant energy.

Extra

Definition: Over-the-top, dramatic, or doing more than what is necessary. While it can be used as a playful critique, being "extra" is also celebrated as a form of unapologetic self-expression.

Example: "She brought five outfit changes to brunch. So extra."

Cultural Note: Gen Z embraces the fun side of being extra, turning it into an art form. After all, life's too short to be boring.

E-girl/E-boy

Definition: Subcultures inspired by emo, anime, and internet aesthetics. E-girls and E-boys are known for their edgy fashion, dramatic makeup, and TikTok-ready looks.
Example: "Her eyeliner is so sharp—total E-girl vibes."
Cultural Note: The "E" stands for "electronic," reflecting their online presence. These aesthetics blend nostalgia and modernity, creating a unique style Gen Z loves.

Eat

Definition: A term used to describe someone excelling or performing exceptionally well.
Example: "She ate that performance—no crumbs left."
Cultural Note: Whether on stage or in life, to "eat" is to dominate with flair and confidence.

Embarrassing

Definition: An exaggerated way of expressing secondhand shame or calling out cringe-worthy behavior. Often said in a playful, sarcastic tone.

Example: "He's still quoting Vine memes in 2024? Embarrassing."

Cultural Note: Gen Z uses this term to point out outdated trends or awkward moments, but it's all in good fun—most of the time.

Emo

Definition: A nostalgic subculture characterized by emotional expression, dark fashion, and angsty music. While rooted in early 2000s culture, "Emo" is enjoying a resurgence thanks to Gen Z's love for retro aesthetics.

Example: "Listening to My Chemical Romance again? I'm back in my Emo phase."

Cultural Note: Emo is more than just an aesthetic; it's a mood. Gen Z has reinvented it with irony and authenticity, proving that emo never truly dies.

Epic

Definition: Something amazing, grand, or unforgettable. While it's been around for decades, "epic" still holds its place in Gen Z vocabulary.
Example: "That party last night was epic."
Cultural Note: Though it's somewhat overused, "epic" remains a go-to descriptor for memorable moments.

Energy

Definition: Used to describe the vibe or attitude someone exudes, often in a complimentary way.
Example: "She walked in with boss energy."
Cultural Note: Gen Z's obsession with "energy" stems from their focus on authenticity and vibes. Whether it's main character energy or chaotic energy, it's all about owning your presence.

Explain Like I'm 5 (ELI5)

Definition: A phrase used online to request a simplified explanation of a complex topic, as though explaining it to a 5-year-old.
Example: "Can someone ELI5 why the stock market crashed?"

Cultural Note: This term reflects Gen Z's desire for clarity and accessibility in a world full of jargon.

Effortlessly Cool

Definition: Describes someone who appears stylish, confident, or charismatic without seeming like they're trying too hard.

Example: "He's got that effortlessly cool vibe—just jeans and a tee, but it works."

Cultural Note: Gen Z loves the idea of authenticity, and "effortlessly cool" embodies their ideal of natural confidence.

Eh

Definition: A versatile filler word or expression of indifference. It can mean "whatever" or be used to downplay something.

Example: "Do you want to go out tonight? Eh, I don't know."

Cultural Note: While it may seem dismissive, "Eh" often reflects Gen Z's laid-back attitude.

Existential Crisis

Definition: A period of deep questioning about life, purpose, or identity. While traditionally serious, Gen Z often uses it humorously to describe everyday stressors.
Example: "I spilled my coffee and now I'm having an existential crisis."
Cultural Note: Turning existential dread into comedy is peak Gen Z—they embrace the chaos of life with humor and memes.

Effort Post

Definition: A social media or forum post that's well-researched, detailed, and thoughtfully written.
Example: "That thread on climate change was an effort post—it had graphs and everything."
Cultural Note: In a world of short attention spans, effort posts are rare gems that stand out for their substance.

F

Fire, Finsta, and the Fabulousness of Gen Z

The letter "F" in Gen Z's dictionary is all about flair, fun, and keeping it fresh. Whether it's hyping someone up with "Fire," expressing realness with "Finsta," or navigating "Friendship Goals," "F" brings a fabulous blend of humor, emotion, and energy. Let's dive into the fierce and fun world of "F."

Fire

Definition: Something amazing, cool, or exceptionally good. Often used to describe outfits, songs, or experiences.
Example: "That jacket is fire—where did you get it?"
Cultural Note: Gen Z took a simple word and turned it into the ultimate stamp of approval. If it's fire, it's worth talking about.

Finsta

Definition: A "fake Instagram" account used to post more personal, unfiltered, or less polished content. It's a space for close friends, away from the curated perfection of a main account.

Example: "Her finsta is hilarious—she's so real on there."

Cultural Note: Finstas reflect Gen Z's duality: polished on the surface but raw and authentic behind the scenes.

Flex

Definition: To show off or boast about something, either sincerely or ironically.

Example: "Not to flex, but I got front-row tickets to the concert."

Cultural Note: Flexing can be a power move or a playful way to share accomplishments. Bonus points if it's paired with humility.

Friendship Goals

Definition: The idealized image of a close, supportive, and often enviable friendship.

Example: "Their TikToks together are pure friendship

goals."

Cultural Note: Gen Z loves celebrating wholesome, unbreakable bonds. Friendship goals are less about competition and more about inspiration.

Fake Deep

Definition: Describes something or someone pretending to be profound or intellectual without actually saying anything meaningful.

Example: "That caption about sunsets and life is so fake deep."

Cultural Note: Gen Z has a low tolerance for pretentiousness and uses "fake deep" to call it out with humor.

Feels

Definition: Short for "feelings," often used to describe an emotional reaction to something, ranging from sadness to nostalgia.

Example: "That movie gave me all the feels."

Cultural Note: Gen Z embraces their emotional side, often sharing moments that hit them right in the feels.

Fam

Definition: Short for "family," but often used to describe close friends or a trusted inner circle.
Example: "What's up, fam?"
Cultural Note: Fam reflects Gen Z's inclusive approach to relationships, where friends are chosen family.

Fake Friend

Definition: Someone who pretends to be supportive or loyal but is actually insincere or unreliable.
Example: "She didn't defend me in that argument. Total fake friend move."
Cultural Note: Gen Z values authenticity in relationships and doesn't hesitate to call out fake friends.

FOMO (Fear of Missing Out)

Definition: The anxiety or regret you feel when you think you're missing out on a fun or exciting event.
Example: "Seeing everyone's stories from the concert

gave me major FOMO."
Cultural Note: While FOMO is universal, Gen Z often counters it with "JOMO" (Joy of Missing Out), embracing self-care over social pressure.

Facts

Definition: Used to agree strongly with a statement or emphasize its truth.
Example: "Pizza is the best comfort food. Facts."
Cultural Note: Straightforward and versatile, "Facts" is Gen Z's way of saying, "You're absolutely right."

Free

Definition: Can mean something is actually free (as in costless) or used ironically to describe someone's availability or willingness to do something.
Example: "I'm free tomorrow if you want to hang out."
Cultural Note: The word's simplicity makes it a staple for quick, casual planning.

Finna

Definition: A slang contraction of "fixing to," meaning "about to" or "going to."
Example: "I'm finna grab some food—you want anything?"
Cultural Note: Popularized in AAVE (African American Vernacular English), "Finna" has become a casual go-to in Gen Z's vocabulary.

Fire Emoji (🔥)

Definition: Used to emphasize how cool, amazing, or exciting something is.
Example: "That photo? Pure 🔥."
Cultural Note: Emojis play a massive role in Gen Z's communication, and the fire emoji is the MVP for hyping things up.

Fake It Till You Make It

Definition: A motivational phrase encouraging confidence and persistence, even when you're unsure.

Example: "I was nervous during the interview, but I just faked it till I made it."

Cultural Note: Gen Z uses this phrase as both genuine advice and a playful acknowledgment of imposter syndrome.

Forever Mood

Definition: A phrase used to describe something or someone that's endlessly relatable or iconic.

Example: "That cat video is a forever mood."

Cultural Note: Gen Z thrives on finding timeless moments of connection, and "Forever Mood" captures this perfectly.

G

Glow-Up, Gaslighting, and Gen Z Greatness

The letter "G" in Gen Z's lexicon is packed with glamour, growth, and a pinch of sarcasm. From celebrating personal transformations ("Glow-Up") to calling out manipulative behavior ("Gaslighting"), this chapter dives into the good, the gritty, and the genius of Gen Z's language. Let's get into the greatness of "G."

Glow-Up

Definition: A significant transformation, often related to appearance or confidence, that highlights improvement or growth.

Example: "After summer break, she had the ultimate glow-up!"

Cultural Note: Glow-ups aren't just about looks; they're about leveling up in all areas of life, and Gen Z celebrates every milestone.

Gaslighting

Definition: A form of manipulation where someone makes another person doubt their perception of reality.
Example: "He kept saying I imagined the text, but I know it happened. That's gaslighting."
Cultural Note: Once a niche psychological term, "Gaslighting" has become a widely used concept for identifying toxic behavior.

Goals

Definition: A term used to describe something admirable, aspirational, or worth striving for.
Example: "That vacation pic is total goals."
Cultural Note: From "friendship goals" to "aesthetic goals," Gen Z uses this word to celebrate inspiration in everyday life.

Go Off

Definition: A phrase used to encourage or hype someone up, especially when they're speaking passionately or acting confidently.

Example: "You aced that presentation—go off, queen!"
Cultural Note: "Go Off" is a verbal high-five, cheering on someone's confidence and energy.

Gucci

Definition: Slang for "good," "cool," or "fine." While it's also a luxury brand, Gen Z has repurposed it into casual slang.
Example: "I'm feeling gucci today—everything's going great!"
Cultural Note: A prime example of how Gen Z gives old slang a fresh twist.

Gatekeeping

Definition: The act of limiting access to information, trends, or communities by excluding others or keeping knowledge exclusive.
Example: "Stop gatekeeping that playlist and share it with us!"
Cultural Note: Gen Z embraces inclusivity and often calls out gatekeeping as unnecessary elitism.

Gassed Up

Definition: Feeling confident or hyped, often because of compliments or encouragement.
Example: "I'm so gassed up after reading all those nice comments."
Cultural Note: Gen Z loves celebrating each other's wins, making "Gassed Up" a term of empowerment.

Good Vibes Only

Definition: A mantra or attitude focusing on positivity and rejecting negativity.
Example: "Leave the drama at home—it's good vibes only here."
Cultural Note: While it's a great sentiment, Gen Z also loves poking fun at overly optimistic "good vibes only" culture.

G.O.A.T. (Greatest of All Time)

Definition: A term used to describe someone or something that's the best at what they do.
Example: "LeBron James is the GOAT of basketball."
Cultural Note: Gen Z uses this acronym across sports, music, and everyday life to celebrate icons and excellence.

Glow

Definition: Radiating positivity, confidence, or happiness. Can be literal (as in glowing skin) or metaphorical.
Example: "She's glowing after getting that promotion."
Cultural Note: Glow is all about celebrating the moments when people truly shine.

Get That Bread

Definition: A motivational phrase encouraging someone to hustle, work hard, or secure financial success.
Example: "Rise and grind—time to get that bread!"
Cultural Note: Bread = money, and Gen Z knows the grind is real, but they'll make it fun.

Girl Boss

Definition: A term celebrating empowered, ambitious women taking charge of their careers or lives.
Example: "She's managing a whole team at 25. Total girl boss."
Cultural Note: While it's meant to be empowering, "Girl Boss" is often used ironically by Gen Z to highlight performative feminism.

Glitch

Definition: A technical error or malfunction. In slang, it can also refer to someone acting oddly or unexpectedly.
Example: "That TikTok video glitched halfway through."
Cultural Note: Gen Z embraces glitches as a quirky part of the digital experience.

Gas

Definition: High praise or excitement about something. Can also refer to hyping someone up.

Example: "That new album is pure gas—I can't stop listening!"

Cultural Note: Whether it's music, fashion, or a vibe, "Gas" means it's worth the hype.

H

High-Key, Hits Different, and the Hype of Gen Z

The letter "H" in Gen Z lingo is where things get heartfelt, hilarious, and hyped. From embracing emotional depth ("Hits Different") to flaunting confidence ("High-Key"), this chapter dives into a collection of words and phrases that highlight the humor and honesty of Gen Z culture. Let's explore the unique charm of "H."

High-Key

Definition: Openly, obviously, or without hesitation. The opposite of "Low-Key." It's used to emphasize something important or exciting.
Example: "I'm high-key obsessed with this show."
Cultural Note: Gen Z uses "High-Key" to bring boldness to their statements, showcasing their love for being unapologetic.

Hits Different

Definition: A phrase used to describe an experience, song, or moment that feels uniquely impactful or emotional.
Example: "Hearing this song while driving at night just hits different."
Cultural Note: This phrase captures Gen Z's ability to articulate the depth of seemingly simple experiences.

Hype

Definition: Excitement, energy, or enthusiasm surrounding a person, event, or thing.
Example: "The hype around that new Marvel movie is real."
Cultural Note: For Gen Z, hype is both an emotion and a movement—it's all about building excitement and sharing it with others.

Hot Girl Summer

Definition: A phrase celebrating confidence, fun, and living your best life during the summer. Originating from rapper Megan Thee Stallion, it's now a mantra for self-empowerment.

Example: "Time to hit the beach—it's Hot Girl Summer!"

Cultural Note: Gen Z embraces this as a state of mind, emphasizing independence and positivity.

Hard Launch

Definition: Publicly revealing a new relationship or project on social media in a bold and unmistakable way.

Example: "She posted their vacation pics—definitely a hard launch of their relationship."

Cultural Note: Contrasts with "Soft Launch," where the reveal is subtle or ambiguous.

Haters

Definition: People who criticize or dislike something, often out of jealousy or misunderstanding.

Example: "Ignore the haters—you're doing great!"

Cultural Note: Gen Z handles haters with humor, often turning their negativity into jokes or motivational fuel.

Hustle Culture

Definition: A mindset focused on constant productivity and striving for success, often at the expense of rest or balance.
Example: "I'm trying to escape hustle culture and focus on self-care instead."
Cultural Note: While Gen Z values ambition, they're also critical of burnout culture and prioritize mental health.

Humble Brag

Definition: A statement that appears modest but is actually meant to draw attention to one's achievements or advantages.
Example: "I'm so exhausted from flying first class all week."
Cultural Note: Gen Z calls out humble brags with humor, preferring authenticity over disguised boasts.

Hard Pass

Definition: A definitive and straightforward way to decline something.
Example: "They suggested pineapple on pizza, and I gave it a hard pass."
Cultural Note: Gen Z loves clarity, and "Hard Pass" is a no-nonsense way to express disinterest.

Hot Take

Definition: An opinion that's bold, controversial, or unconventional.
Example: "Hot take: Oat milk is overrated."
Cultural Note: Gen Z thrives on hot takes, using them to spark debate, share humor, or challenge norms.

Hypebeast

Definition: Someone who's obsessed with trendy fashion, especially exclusive streetwear or sneaker brands.
Example: "He's such a hypebeast with those limited-edition Jordans."
Cultural Note: While admired for their dedication to

style, hypebeasts can also be teased for their obsession with labels.

Haunt

Definition: Refers to the lingering presence of something, whether it's a thought, memory, or even a social media post.
Example: "That embarrassing tweet from 2016 still haunts me."
Cultural Note: Gen Z's humor often embraces the haunting nature of their digital footprints.

Head Empty

Definition: A phrase used humorously to describe a lack of thought or focus, often in a carefree or overwhelmed context.
Example: "I forgot my homework—head empty, no thoughts."
Cultural Note: Reflects Gen Z's self-aware humor about moments of mental blankness.

I

Iconic, IYKYK, and the Irresistible Charm of Gen Z

The letter "I" in Gen Z's lexicon is bursting with individuality and intrigue. From celebrating timeless greatness ("Iconic") to embracing exclusivity with a wink ("IYKYK"), this chapter explores the influential and imaginative side of Gen Z's vocabulary. Let's illuminate the innovative world of "I."

Iconic

Definition: Something or someone universally admired for being legendary, memorable, or groundbreaking.
Example: "Her outfit at the Met Gala was so iconic."
Cultural Note: Gen Z uses "Iconic" not just to describe grand achievements but also quirky, relatable moments that stand out.

IYKYK (If You Know, You Know)

Definition: A cryptic phrase used to reference inside jokes, niche knowledge, or experiences understood only by a select group.

Example: "That concert last night… IYKYK."

Cultural Note: This acronym embodies Gen Z's love for creating intimate, exclusive connections in a hyperconnected world.

It's Giving…

Definition: A phrase used to describe the vibe or energy something is projecting, often followed by a specific comparison.

Example: "Her look is giving CEO realness."

Cultural Note: Flexible and dramatic, this phrase lets Gen Z creatively convey impressions with flair.

In My Feels

Definition: A state of emotional vulnerability, often brought on by a song, movie, or memory.

Example: "This rainy weather has me in my feels."

Cultural Note: Gen Z isn't afraid to own their emotions, and "In My Feels" is the perfect shorthand for sharing them.

Instant Regret

Definition: A humorous way to describe the immediate realization of a bad decision.
Example: "I tried that spicy challenge, and it was instant regret."
Cultural Note: Reflecting Gen Z's self-aware humor, this phrase turns mistakes into relatable content.

Internet Famous

Definition: Achieving celebrity status through viral content or social media.
Example: "She went internet famous after that TikTok blew up."
Cultural Note: Gen Z celebrates the power of digital platforms to create stars overnight, redefining fame in the process.

IRL (In Real Life)

Definition: Used to contrast online interactions with physical, face-to-face experiences.
Example: "We've been texting for weeks, but we're finally meeting IRL."
Cultural Note: As digital natives, Gen Z values both online connections and the authenticity of IRL moments.

Ice

Definition: Slang for expensive jewelry, often diamonds or other sparkly accessories.
Example: "Check out all that ice on his wrist!"
Cultural Note: Reflecting luxury and success, "Ice" is a symbol of achievement and style.

It's Not That Deep

Definition: A phrase used to downplay drama or overthinking.
Example: "Relax, it's not that deep—it's just a meme."
Cultural Note: Gen Z's way of reminding themselves and others to keep things in perspective.

I Can't Even

Definition: An expression of being overwhelmed, speechless, or amused, often left unfinished for dramatic effect.
Example: "Did you see that viral cat video? I can't even!"
Cultural Note: Perfectly encapsulates moments when words fail but emotions run high.

Influencer

Definition: A social media personality with the power to sway opinions, trends, and purchasing decisions.
Example: "She's my favorite beauty influencer."
Cultural Note: Influencers are modern-day celebrities, blending relatability with aspirational content to connect with Gen Z.

Insta-Worthy

Definition: Describes something so visually appealing that it's perfect for posting on Instagram.
Example: "This latte art is totally Insta-worthy."
Cultural Note: Gen Z's eye for aesthetics ensures that Insta-worthy moments are everywhere, from travel shots to daily routines.

Is That a Threat or a Promise?

Definition: A playful or sarcastic response to an ambiguous or bold statement.
Example: "If you eat my fries, I'm taking yours." "Is that a threat or a promise?"
Cultural Note: Highlights Gen Z's love for turning everyday banter into humor.

J

JOMO, Juice, and the Joyful Jargon of Gen Z

The letter "J" in Gen Z's dictionary is all about balancing carefree joy with sharp social commentary. From celebrating the pleasure of missing out ("JOMO") to discussing influence and reputation ("Juice"), this chapter dives into a diverse mix of phrases and words that showcase Gen Z's wit, wisdom, and whimsical side. Let's jump into the jubilant world of "J."

JOMO (Joy of Missing Out)

Definition: The opposite of FOMO (Fear of Missing Out), it's the contentment and relief that comes from choosing to skip social events or activities.

Example: "Everyone's at the party, but I'm home watching Netflix with snacks. JOMO for real."

Cultural Note: JOMO reflects Gen Z's embrace of self-care and intentional living over societal pressures to always participate.

Juice

Definition: Influence, reputation, or clout; being well-respected or admired.

Example: "He's got the juice—everyone listens to his ideas."

Cultural Note: Juice can also refer to someone's charisma or energy, making it a versatile term for highlighting greatness.

Just Vibes

Definition: A phrase used to describe a relaxed, carefree atmosphere or approach to life.

Example: "No plans tonight—just vibes."

Cultural Note: Gen Z uses "Just Vibes" to emphasize living in the moment and letting go of unnecessary stress.

Joke's on You

Definition: A witty comeback or statement used when someone's attempt to insult or outsmart you backfires.

Example: "You thought I'd be upset? Joke's on you—I

don't care."

Cultural Note: Gen Z loves flipping the script with humor, and "Joke's on You" is a classic way to do it.

JK (Just Kidding)

Definition: A lighthearted phrase or abbreviation used to clarify that a statement was a joke.

Example: "I'm moving to Mars. JK, but wouldn't that be cool?"

Cultural Note: While it's been around for decades, "JK" remains a staple in Gen Z's casual conversations and text messages.

Jinx

Definition: A playful term used when two people say the same thing at the same time, often followed by a friendly game where the jinxed person can't speak until their name is said.

Example: "We both said 'pizza' at the same time—jinx!"

Cultural Note: Jinx remains a nostalgic, fun moment of synchronicity in Gen Z interactions.

Jump Scare

Definition: Originally a term from horror movies, it's now used humorously to describe sudden, unexpected, or shocking things.
Example: "That old yearbook photo of me? Total jump scare."
Cultural Note: Gen Z's use of "Jump Scare" reflects their love for dramatizing everyday moments with humor.

Just Saying

Definition: A phrase used to add emphasis to a statement, often to express an opinion or observation without sounding too harsh.
Example: "You might want to double-check your math… just saying."
Cultural Note: This phrase allows Gen Z to share their thoughts while maintaining a laid-back tone.

Jaded

Definition: Feeling disillusioned or cynical, often after experiencing too much of something.
Example: "After so many failed auditions, I'm a little jaded about the industry."
Cultural Note: While being jaded isn't exclusive to Gen Z, they've perfected the art of expressing it with a blend of humor and honesty.

Juice Cleanse

Definition: A detox or health trend where someone consumes only juice for a set period. Used literally or humorously to describe self-improvement attempts.
Example: "I'm doing a mental juice cleanse—no social media this weekend."
Cultural Note: Gen Z often uses health trends like "Juice Cleanse" as metaphors for broader life resets.

Jumping on the Bandwagon

Definition: Joining a popular trend, movement, or activity, often after it's already gained momentum.
Example: "Everyone's jumping on the bandwagon for this new show."

Cultural Note: Gen Z isn't afraid to call out bandwagon behavior but also recognizes the fun in collective experiences.

Juggle the Drama

Definition: A phrase used to describe managing or navigating chaotic social situations or conflicts.
Example: "Group chats are wild—I'm constantly juggling the drama."
Cultural Note: Gen Z's social lives often include overlapping digital and real-world interactions, making "juggling drama" a relatable skill.

K

Keeping It 100, Kinda Obsessed, and the Key to Gen Z Coolness

---

The letter "K" in Gen Z's dictionary brings a kaleidoscope of words and phrases that capture authenticity, enthusiasm, and humor. From expressing sincerity ("Keeping It 100") to celebrating casual obsession ("Kinda Obsessed"), "K" reflects a dynamic mix of confidence and chill. Let's crack open the quirky and cool world of "K."

Keeping It 100

Definition: Being honest, real, or authentic. It's about staying true to yourself or others.
Example: "I'll keep it 100—that outfit isn't your best look."
Cultural Note: Gen Z values transparency and sincerity, and "Keeping It 100" is their stamp of approval for genuine vibes.

Kinda Obsessed

Definition: A playful way to admit you really like or enjoy something, without sounding overly dramatic.
Example: "This new album? I'm kinda obsessed."
Cultural Note: Perfectly encapsulates Gen Z's love for casual enthusiasm and low-key fandoms.

Killin' It

Definition: Doing an amazing job, excelling, or dominating a situation.
Example: "You're killin' it with those dance moves!"
Cultural Note: A hype phrase that Gen Z uses to uplift and celebrate others.

Keyboard Warrior

Definition: Someone who aggressively argues or debates online, often with little regard for tact or consequences.
Example: "Don't listen to the keyboard warriors in the comments."
Cultural Note: Gen Z is keenly aware of the toxicity of online debates and often uses humor to call it out.

Kiki

Definition: A fun, lighthearted gathering or hangout, often with close friends.
Example: "Let's have a kiki this weekend and catch up!"
Cultural Note: Borrowed from LGBTQ+ culture, "Kiki" emphasizes inclusivity and joy in social interactions.

Karma

Definition: The concept that actions, good or bad, eventually come back to you. Used literally or humorously.
Example: "She got caught lying? That's karma for you."
Cultural Note: Gen Z loves referencing karma as a way to balance humor and accountability.

Kickback

Definition: A casual, laid-back gathering or party.
Example: "Nothing crazy tonight—just a small kickback

at my place."
Cultural Note: Gen Z uses "Kickback" to describe low-pressure socializing, valuing chill vibes over extravagant parties.

Know Your Worth

Definition: A phrase encouraging self-respect, confidence, and not settling for less than you deserve.
Example: "Don't answer his 2 a.m. texts—know your worth!"
Cultural Note: Gen Z uses this phrase as both empowerment and a playful call-out for self-awareness.

Knocked It Out of the Park

Definition: A metaphor meaning to excel or exceed expectations.
Example: "Your presentation today? You knocked it out of the park!"
Cultural Note: Though it's an older phrase, Gen Z uses it with flair to hype each other up.

Keyboard Smash

Definition: Randomly hitting keys to express excitement, frustration, or overwhelming emotion online.
Example: "That movie ending had me like ajdkfjskdf!!!"
Cultural Note: The ultimate Gen Z way of capturing big feelings in small moments.

Kings and Queens

Definition: Terms of endearment or praise, often used to hype someone up or acknowledge their worth.
Example: "Go off, queen! You're amazing."
Cultural Note: Celebrating individuality and empowerment, these words reflect Gen Z's love for uplifting language.

Know-It-All

Definition: Someone who acts like they know everything, often in an annoying or arrogant way.
Example: "He kept correcting everyone during the meeting—such a know-it-all."

Cultural Note: While Gen Z appreciates confidence, they're quick to call out over-the-top arrogance with humor.

L

Lit, Low-Key, and the Legendary Lingo of Gen Z

The letter "L" in Gen Z's vocabulary is all about keeping it light, laid-back, and legendary. Whether it's celebrating excitement with "Lit," embracing chill energy with "Low-Key," or dealing with losses ("L"), "L" showcases a wide range of expressions that perfectly capture the highs and lows of modern life. Let's explore the lively language of "L."

Lit

Definition: Something exciting, fun, or amazing; can also describe a lively event or situation.
Example: "That concert last night was so lit!"
Cultural Note: One of the most iconic Gen Z terms, "Lit" reflects a generation's love for celebrating memorable moments with enthusiasm.

Low-Key

Definition: Subtle, understated, or not overly dramatic. It's used to downplay something or express a mild opinion.

Example: "I'm low-key obsessed with this new show."

Cultural Note: Gen Z's preference for chill vibes is perfectly encapsulated in "Low-Key." Its versatility makes it a go-to in casual conversations.

L

Definition: Short for "loss," it's used to describe a failure, mistake, or disappointing situation.

Example: "I missed the bus this morning—huge L."

Cultural Note: While "L" might sound negative, Gen Z often uses it humorously to brush off minor setbacks.

Let's Go

Definition: A phrase expressing excitement, hype, or motivation, often used to celebrate a success or rally a group.

Example: "You got the job? Let's go!"

Cultural Note: Gen Z's love for hyping each other up shines through this simple yet powerful phrase.

Live Rent-Free

Definition: Refers to something or someone that occupies your thoughts frequently, whether positively or negatively.
Example: "That TikTok sound lives rent-free in my head."
Cultural Note: Reflecting Gen Z's playful self-awareness, this phrase highlights their ability to turn even their own mental distractions into humor.

Love That for You

Definition: A supportive or sometimes sarcastic way of expressing happiness for someone else.
Example: "You're going on vacation again? Love that for you!"
Cultural Note: While often genuine, the tone can shift based on context, adding a layer of playful ambiguity.

Left On Read

Definition: When someone reads your message but doesn't reply, leaving you hanging.
Example: "He left me on read all day—rude!"
Cultural Note: A relatable digital experience, "Left On Read" encapsulates the highs and lows of online communication.

Literally

Definition: Used to emphasize a point, even when the statement isn't literal.
Example: "I'm literally dying over how funny that video is."
Cultural Note: Gen Z's use of "Literally" blends exaggeration with humor, making it both expressive and entertaining.

Let Them Cook

Definition: A phrase meaning to give someone the space to work, perform, or prove themselves.
Example: "I know his strategy seems weird, but let him cook."
Cultural Note: Often used humorously, this phrase

reflects Gen Z's tendency to cheer on unconventional approaches.

Level Up

Definition: To improve, grow, or reach the next stage of success.
Example: "She really leveled up with that new job."
Cultural Note: Gen Z embraces self-improvement and uses "Level Up" as a motivational mantra for achieving goals.

Lost Cause

Definition: Someone or something deemed beyond help or repair.
Example: "Trying to fix my sleep schedule is a lost cause."
Cultural Note: Often said with humor, "Lost Cause" highlights Gen Z's ability to find levity in life's challenges.

Late Night Feels

Definition: Emotional thoughts or reflections that hit hardest at night, often when you're alone.

Example: "I was deep in my late-night feels thinking about old memories."

Cultural Note: Gen Z's embrace of emotional vulnerability shines through phrases like this.

M

Main Character Energy, Mood, and the Magic of Gen Z

The letter "M" in Gen Z's dictionary is a masterclass in self-expression, relatability, and motivation. From embracing the spotlight ("Main Character Energy") to perfectly capturing a vibe ("Mood"), "M" delivers a mix of humor, empowerment, and emotional depth. Let's dive into the meaningful and magical language of "M."

Main Character Energy

Definition: The confidence and charisma of someone who acts as if they are the protagonist in their life story.
Example: "Walking through the park with my iced coffee—I'm giving main character energy today."
Cultural Note: This phrase highlights Gen Z's focus on self-love, individuality, and owning one's narrative.

Mood

Definition: A term used to express relatability or agreement with something that captures a feeling or vibe.

Example: "That picture of the dog wrapped in a blanket? Mood."

Cultural Note: Simple yet powerful, "Mood" is the quintessential Gen Z shorthand for shared experiences and emotions.

Mid

Definition: Used to describe something mediocre, average, or underwhelming.

Example: "That movie everyone hyped up? It was so mid."

Cultural Note: Gen Z isn't afraid to call out when things don't meet expectations, and "Mid" is their way of keeping it real.

Manifest

Definition: To focus on positive thoughts or actions in order to bring about a desired outcome.

Example: "I'm manifesting good vibes for this job

interview."

Cultural Note: Rooted in the law of attraction, Gen Z embraces "Manifest" as a blend of optimism and self-empowerment.

Miss Me with That

Definition: A phrase used to dismiss something unwanted, irrelevant, or unappealing.
Example: "Another meeting that could've been an email? Miss me with that."
Cultural Note: Gen Z's ability to cut through nonsense with humor shines through in this phrase.

Mainstream

Definition: Popular, widely accepted, or conventional; often used critically to describe trends that lack originality.
Example: "That band used to be cool, but now they're so mainstream."
Cultural Note: Gen Z values authenticity and often calls out mainstream trends that feel overly commercialized.

Mood Board

Definition: A visual collage or collection of images and ideas used to inspire creativity or set a specific aesthetic.
Example: "I made a mood board for my dream apartment decor."
Cultural Note: Whether digital or physical, mood boards reflect Gen Z's love for aesthetics and personalization.

Muted

Definition: Silencing someone on social media without unfollowing them, often to avoid drama or overly frequent posts.
Example: "I muted her stories—she posts like 20 times a day."
Cultural Note: Gen Z values digital boundaries and uses tools like "Mute" to curate their online experiences.

Main Character Moment

Definition: A specific instance where someone feels like the star of their own life story.

Example: "When I caught the bouquet at the wedding—total main character moment."

Cultural Note: This phrase celebrates everyday victories and standout experiences with a touch of cinematic flair.

Mentally I'm Here

Definition: A phrase used to describe where someone's thoughts or dreams are, often paired with an image of an idyllic or humorous place.

Example: "Physically I'm at work, but mentally I'm on a beach in Bali."

Cultural Note: Highlights Gen Z's tendency to balance reality with escapism through humor.

Microdosing

Definition: Originally a term for consuming small amounts of psychedelics, it's now humorously used to describe enjoying small doses of everyday pleasures.

Example: "I'm microdosing happiness with these tiny chocolates."

Mid-Tier

Definition: A step above "mid," but not exceptional; something decent but not great.
Example: "The food wasn't bad, but it was definitely mid-tier."
Cultural Note: This phrase reflects Gen Z's nuanced approach to evaluating quality.

N

No Cap, Niche, and the Nuanced Narratives of Gen Z

The letter "N" in Gen Z's dictionary is packed with honesty, individuality, and creative twists. From expressing sincerity ("No Cap") to highlighting unique corners of the internet ("Niche"), "N" captures the nuanced and sometimes quirky ways Gen Z communicates. Let's navigate the notable and novel language of "N."

No Cap

Definition: A phrase meaning "no lie" or "I'm being honest," often used to emphasize the truthfulness of a statement.
Example: "That pizza was the best I've ever had, no cap."
Cultural Note: "No Cap" reflects Gen Z's commitment to authenticity and their aversion to pretense.

Niche

Definition: Refers to a highly specific interest, community, or area of expertise, often celebrated for its uniqueness.
Example: "She's really into vintage keyboard collecting—such a niche hobby."
Cultural Note: Gen Z's embrace of "Niche" highlights their love for individuality and finding joy in the oddly specific.

Netflix and Chill

Definition: Originally a phrase for watching Netflix in a relaxed setting, it's now commonly used as a euphemism for romantic or intimate time.
Example: "He invited me over to Netflix and chill."
Cultural Note: While lighthearted, the phrase also reflects Gen Z's playful approach to social interactions.

Not Me

Definition: A humorous or self-deprecating way to admit to doing something embarrassing or relatable.

Example: "Not me eating a whole pint of ice cream at 2 a.m."

Cultural Note: Often paired with memes or GIFs, "Not Me" is a staple in Gen Z's self-aware humor.

NGL (Not Gonna Lie)

Definition: A phrase used to preface an honest or blunt statement.

Example: "NGL, I didn't study for this test at all."

Cultural Note: Gen Z uses "NGL" to create a tone of casual honesty in conversations.

Neutral

Definition: Describes someone or something that is unbiased, calm, or not taking sides.

Example: "I'm staying neutral in this group chat drama."

Cultural Note: Neutrality is valued by Gen Z, especially in social dynamics where they prefer avoiding unnecessary conflict.

Not the...

Definition: A phrase used to call out or emphasize something ironic, unexpected, or ridiculous.
Example: "Not the dog wearing sunglasses at the park!"
Cultural Note: "Not the..." phrases reflect Gen Z's humor, which thrives on pointing out absurdities with dramatic flair.

No Thoughts, Head Empty

Definition: A humorous way to describe a blank mental state, often used to poke fun at oneself.
Example: "I walked into the room and forgot why—no thoughts, head empty."
Cultural Note: This phrase reflects Gen Z's love for turning everyday brain farts into relatable content.

Name-Drop

Definition: Casually mentioning someone famous or important to impress others.

Example: "He name-dropped three celebrities he met at Coachella."
Cultural Note: While often seen as a flex, Gen Z also uses "Name-Drop" ironically to mock pretentious behavior.

Niche Internet Microcelebrity

Definition: Someone with a modest but devoted online following, often within a specific niche or community.
Example: "She's a niche internet microcelebrity in the slime-making world."
Cultural Note: This phrase highlights how Gen Z's digital culture allows anyone to build influence, no matter how obscure their interests.

Never Not

Definition: A playful double negative used to emphasize something consistent or true.
Example: "She's never not early to every meeting."
Cultural Note: Gen Z loves turning phrases for dramatic or humorous effect, and "Never Not" is a perfect example.

No Chill

Definition: Describes someone who's overly dramatic, excitable, or lacking self-control.
Example: "He roasted me for one typo—he's got no chill."
Cultural Note: While it can be a playful critique, "No Chill" is also a way to call out unnecessary intensity.

O

On Fleek, Over It, and the Optimistic Outbursts of Gen Z

The letter "O" in Gen Z's dictionary reflects a mix of trendsetting expressions, emotional honesty, and lighthearted humor. From perfect brows ("On Fleek") to hitting emotional thresholds ("Over It"), this chapter captures how Gen Z navigates style, vibes, and relatable moments. Let's open the outstanding world of "O."

On Fleek

Definition: Perfectly styled, on point, or looking exceptionally good.
Example: "Her eyebrows are on fleek today!"
Cultural Note: Popularized in the mid-2010s, "On Fleek" remains a nostalgic yet iconic phrase that embodies peak aesthetic achievement.

Over It

Definition: Feeling done, annoyed, or completely finished with something.

Example: "This group project is taking forever—I'm so over it."

Cultural Note: A succinct way for Gen Z to express frustration while keeping it casual.

Oof

Definition: An exclamation used to express sympathy, embarrassment, or acknowledgment of a difficult situation.

Example: "You forgot your homework? Oof, that sucks."

Cultural Note: Originating from gaming culture (notably Roblox), "Oof" has become a universal reaction word.

OK Boomer

Definition: A dismissive phrase used to call out outdated or irrelevant opinions, often from older generations.

Example: "You don't understand memes? OK Boomer."

Cultural Note: While it started as a clapback, "OK

Boomer" reflects Gen Z's humor and critique of generational differences.

On God

Definition: A phrase used to emphasize sincerity or truthfulness.
Example: "I'm telling you, this movie is amazing—on God."
Cultural Note: Often paired with strong statements, "On God" is Gen Z's way of doubling down on their conviction.

Out of Pocket

Definition: Acting unexpectedly, inappropriate, or wild.
Example: "He said what in the group chat? That's out of pocket."
Cultural Note: Originally referring to being unreachable, Gen Z has redefined this phrase to call out unpredictable behavior.

On Repeat

Definition: Refers to something, usually a song, that's being played continuously because it's so good.
Example: "This new track is fire—it's been on repeat all day."
Cultural Note: Reflects Gen Z's passion for sharing their favorite media and obsessing over quality content.

Online Sleuthing

Definition: Investigating or researching someone or something using social media or the internet.
Example: "I met someone new, so naturally I did some online sleuthing."
Cultural Note: A skill many Gen Zers have mastered, often used playfully or for practical purposes.

OMG

Definition: Short for "Oh My God," an exclamation of surprise, excitement, or disbelief.
Example: "OMG, I can't believe we got tickets!"

Cultural Note: A timeless acronym that continues to thrive in text and verbal communication.

Own It

Definition: A phrase encouraging confidence and self-assurance, especially in challenging situations.
Example: "You made a mistake, but just own it and move on."
Cultural Note: Gen Z values accountability and authenticity, and "Own It" reflects that ethos.

P

Periodt, Pull Up, and the Playful Precision of Gen Z

The letter "P" in Gen Z's dictionary represents confidence, clarity, and creativity. Whether it's putting an exclamation point on a statement ("Periodt") or showing readiness ("Pull Up"), "P" offers playful yet precise ways to communicate. Let's explore the power-packed world of "P."

Periodt

Definition: An emphatic way to end a statement, signaling that there's no room for debate.
Example: "I'm the best at Mario Kart. Periodt."
Cultural Note: The added "t" emphasizes finality and flair, often used for dramatic or humorous effect.

Pull Up

Definition: To arrive or show up, often in a casual or confident manner.
Example: "We're at the park—pull up!"
Cultural Note: Gen Z's way of inviting someone to join in the moment, reflecting their spontaneous social dynamics.

Pushin' P

Definition: A phrase popularized in hip-hop culture meaning to keep things positive, real, or player (cool).
Example: "Helping your friends out? That's pushin' P."
Cultural Note: The phrase showcases Gen Z's ability to adapt cultural influences into everyday slang.

Petty

Definition: Being intentionally minorly spiteful or holding onto small grievances for humorous effect.
Example: "He unfollowed me, so I blocked him. Call me petty, I don't care."
Cultural Note: Petty behavior is often exaggerated for laughs, making it a staple of Gen Z humor.

Pick Me

Definition: A term for someone seeking validation by acting overly agreeable or self-deprecating, often at the expense of others.
Example: "She's always saying she's 'not like other girls.' Total pick me vibes."
Cultural Note: Gen Z uses "Pick Me" to critique performative behavior while advocating for authenticity.

Periodt

Definition: Used to emphasize a point or agreement, often in a more neutral or straightforward way than "Periodt."
Example: "We're going out tonight, period."
Cultural Note: Reflects Gen Z's love for creating definitive, bold statements.

PFP (Profile Picture)

Definition: Refers to someone's avatar or profile photo on social media or gaming platforms.

Example: "That PFP is hilarious—where did you find it?"

Cultural Note: With meme culture thriving, PFPs often become extensions of Gen Z's humor and identity.

Pass the Vibe Check

Definition: To align with the mood, energy, or expectations of a group or situation.

Example: "Her outfit totally passes the vibe check."

Cultural Note: A phrase born from TikTok, it's all about fitting in without trying too hard.

Pre-Gaming

Definition: Socializing or drinking before going to a larger event or party.

Example: "We're pre-gaming at my place before the concert."

Cultural Note: While not unique to Gen Z, pre-gaming reflects their emphasis on building excitement and camaraderie.

Pog

Definition: A slang term meaning "awesome" or "exciting," originating from gaming culture.
Example: "You won the match? Pog!"
Cultural Note: "Pog" demonstrates Gen Z's ability to bring niche gaming terms into mainstream slang.

Positive Vibes Only

Definition: A mantra or mindset focused on optimism and avoiding negativity.
Example: "This vacation is all about positive vibes only."
Cultural Note: While aspirational, Gen Z often playfully critiques overly forced positivity.

Photodump

Definition: A casual, uncurated collection of photos posted on social media, often capturing random or candid moments.

Example: "Here's my weekend photodump—swipe for chaos."
Cultural Note: Reflects Gen Z's embrace of authenticity and rejection of overly polished online personas.

Pass

Definition: To decline or say no to something, often with a touch of finality.
Example: "Another horror movie? Hard pass."
Cultural Note: Straightforward and effective, "Pass" is Gen Z's way of setting boundaries with ease.

Q

Queen, Quiet Quitting, and the Quintessential Gen Z Quirks

The letter "Q" in Gen Z's dictionary captures bold empowerment and thought-provoking trends. From celebrating confidence ("Queen") to redefining work-life balance ("Quiet Quitting"), this chapter dives into the quirky and quintessential expressions that shape how Gen Z navigates life. Let's uncover the unique language of "Q."

Queen

Definition: A term of endearment and empowerment used to praise someone's confidence, achievements, or style.
Example: "You aced that presentation—go off, queen!"
Cultural Note: Rooted in LGBTQ+ culture, "Queen" has become a universal Gen Z phrase celebrating individuality and strength.

Quiet Quitting

Definition: Doing the minimum required at work without overextending oneself, often as a way to maintain work-life balance.
Example: "I'm not staying late anymore—quiet quitting is my vibe."
Cultural Note: Reflecting Gen Z's focus on mental health and boundaries, "Quiet Quitting" critiques hustle culture.

Quaking

Definition: A dramatic expression of being shocked, overwhelmed, or impressed.
Example: "Her outfit was so good, I'm quaking."
Cultural Note: Gen Z uses "Quaking" to exaggerate reactions, adding humor and drama to everyday moments.

Quick Flex

Definition: A casual or subtle way of showing off something impressive.

Example: "Just a quick flex—I got front-row tickets to the concert."

Cultural Note: Gen Z embraces "Quick Flex" as a fun and lighthearted way to share achievements without being boastful.

QRT (Quote Retweet)

Definition: Sharing someone's tweet while adding your own commentary or reaction.

Example: "His QRT of that meme was hilarious!"

Cultural Note: A staple of Twitter culture, QRTs let Gen Z remix and amplify online conversations.

Questionable

Definition: Used to describe something that seems odd, off, or suspicious.

Example: "That sushi place has a 2-star review? Questionable."

Cultural Note: Gen Z often uses this term humorously to call out things that don't quite add up.

Quit Playing

Definition: A phrase urging someone to stop joking or being unserious.
Example: "You think pineapple belongs on pizza? Quit playing."
Cultural Note: Reflects Gen Z's love for playful banter and direct communication.

Quality Time

Definition: Meaningful, focused time spent with loved ones or friends.
Example: "This weekend is all about quality time with my besties."
Cultural Note: For Gen Z, quality time often balances screen-free interactions with shared digital experiences.

Quick Question

Definition: A phrase used to preface a casual inquiry, often in texts or emails.

Example: "Quick question: Are we meeting at 2 or 3?"

Cultural Note: While it implies brevity, "Quick Question" sometimes leads to longer conversations, showcasing Gen Z's efficient yet curious nature.

R

Receipts, Rizz, and the Raw Realness of Gen Z

The letter "R" in Gen Z's dictionary brings a rich mix of accountability, charm, and relatability. From proving a point with "Receipts" to showcasing flirtation skills with "Rizz," "R" perfectly captures Gen Z's creative and candid communication style. Let's reveal the remarkable world of "R."

Receipts

Definition: Evidence or proof, often in the form of screenshots or saved messages, used to back up a claim.
Example: "She said she never said that, but I have the receipts."
Cultural Note: In an era of instant communication, "Receipts" emphasize accountability and the importance of keeping receipts (literally and figuratively).

Rizz

Definition: Slang for charm or charisma, particularly when it comes to flirting or attracting others.

Example: "He's got so much rizz—he can talk to anyone."

Cultural Note: Popularized on social media, "Rizz" reflects Gen Z's playful approach to describing social skills.

Real One

Definition: A term of respect for someone who is loyal, genuine, or trustworthy.

Example: "Thanks for always having my back—you're a real one."

Cultural Note: Gen Z values authenticity, and "Real One" is the ultimate compliment for meaningful connections.

Relatable

Definition: Describing something that feels familiar, relevant, or reflective of shared experiences.

Example: "That meme about procrastinating is so relatable."

Cultural Note: Relatability drives Gen Z humor and content creation, fostering connection through shared experiences.

Red Flag

Definition: A warning sign or indication of problematic behavior in someone or something.
Example: "He doesn't like dogs? Major red flag."
Cultural Note: Highlighting potential issues, "Red Flag" is often used humorously or as a cautionary note.

Ratio

Definition: A term used on social media when a reply gets more likes than the original post, often as a sign of disagreement or better engagement.
Example: "That take was so bad, it got ratioed instantly."
Cultural Note: "Ratio" reflects Gen Z's emphasis on collective opinion and the dynamics of online discourse.

Respectfully

Definition: A qualifier used to soften a blunt or potentially offensive statement.
Example: "Respectfully, that outfit is not it."
Cultural Note: Gen Z uses "Respectfully" to add humor or irony while maintaining conversational tone.

Receipts or It Didn't Happen

Definition: A humorous demand for proof when someone makes a bold or unbelievable claim.
Example: "You met Harry Styles? Receipts or it didn't happen!"
Cultural Note: Highlights Gen Z's skepticism and demand for verifiable truths in a digital age.

Rise and Grind

Definition: A motivational phrase encouraging productivity and hustle, often used ironically.
Example: "Another Monday, time to rise and grind... or not."

Cultural Note: While Gen Z values ambition, they often critique hustle culture with humor and self-awareness.

Random

Definition: Something unexpected, unplanned, or odd. Often used to describe quirky or surprising moments.
Example: "That raccoon meme you sent me was so random."
Cultural Note: Gen Z embraces randomness as part of their love for absurd humor and unexpected connections.

S

Slay, Simp, and the Stunning Style of Gen Z Speak

The letter "S" in Gen Z's dictionary is all about confidence, creativity, and connection. From expressing admiration ("Slay") to poking fun at over-the-top behavior ("Simp"), this chapter dives into the stylish and savvy ways Gen Z communicates. Let's step into the spectacular world of "S."

Slay

Definition: To excel, impress, or perform exceptionally well; often used as a compliment for style or achievements.
Example: "You're absolutely slaying in that outfit!"
Cultural Note: Gen Z uses "Slay" to hype others up and celebrate moments of greatness.

Simp

Definition: Someone who does too much for someone they have a crush on, often to the point of losing self-respect.

Example: "He bought her coffee every day for a month and she's not even interested—such a simp."

Cultural Note: While "Simp" is used humorously, it's also a critique of unbalanced relationships or excessive admiration.

Savage

Definition: Bold, fearless, or unapologetically honest; often used to describe someone who delivers a sharp comeback or takes daring actions.

Example: "That clapback was savage."

Cultural Note: Gen Z's love for drama and sharp humor is perfectly captured in this word.

Snack

Definition: A term to describe someone who is physically attractive; they look good enough to "eat."

Example: "He's such a snack in that suit."

Cultural Note: Gen Z's playful approach to flirting and compliments is evident in this tasty metaphor.

Stan

Definition: To be an enthusiastic fan of someone or something; also used as a noun to describe such a fan.
Example: "I stan Taylor Swift so hard."
Cultural Note: Borrowed from Eminem's song "Stan," the term reflects Gen Z's passion for fandom culture.

Spill the Tea

Definition: To share gossip or reveal juicy information.
Example: "You have to spill the tea about what happened at the party."
Cultural Note: Gen Z's love for drama and storytelling makes "Spill the Tea" a conversational favorite.

Soft Launch

Definition: A subtle or understated way of revealing something new, such as a relationship or project.

Example: "That Instagram story of their hands holding is definitely a soft launch."

Cultural Note: Contrasts with "Hard Launch," reflecting Gen Z's nuanced approach to sharing life updates.

Sus

Definition: Short for "suspicious," often used to call out questionable behavior.

Example: "You're being really sus about where you were last night."

Cultural Note: Popularized by the game Among Us, "Sus" has become a staple in Gen Z slang.

Squad Goals

Definition: A phrase used to describe an aspirational or enviable group dynamic among friends.

Example: "Their group photos are pure squad goals."

Cultural Note: Reflects Gen Z's celebration of close-knit friendships and shared aesthetics.

Slept On

Definition: Something or someone underrated or not getting the attention they deserve.
Example: "That indie movie is so slept on."
Cultural Note: Gen Z loves shining a light on hidden gems and underappreciated talent.

Send It

Definition: A phrase encouraging someone to go for it, take a risk, or fully commit to an action.
Example: "You're thinking about cliff diving? Just send it!"
Cultural Note: Reflects Gen Z's adventurous spirit and love for spontaneous decisions.

T

Thirsty, Throwing Shade, and the Trendy Talk of Gen Z

The letter "T" in Gen Z's dictionary is filled with sass, humor, and cultural relevance. From seeking attention ("Thirsty") to subtle disses ("Throwing Shade"), "T" captures the vibrant and creative communication style of this generation. Let's tap into the thrilling and trendy world of "T."

Thirsty

Definition: Desperate for attention, validation, or affection, often in a humorous or exaggerated sense.
Example: "He keeps liking all her posts—so thirsty."
Cultural Note: While often playful, "Thirsty" can also point out over-the-top attempts to get noticed.

Throwing Shade

Definition: Subtly or indirectly insulting or criticizing someone.

Example: "That comment about my outfit was definitely throwing shade."

Cultural Note: A staple in Gen Z humor, "Throwing Shade" is about wit and subtlety over outright confrontation.

TL;DR (Too Long; Didn't Read)

Definition: A brief summary of a longer text or situation, often used to save time.

Example: "TL;DR: The movie was great, but the ending was confusing."

Cultural Note: Reflecting Gen Z's need for efficiency in a world of information overload.

The Tea

Definition: Gossip or juicy information, often shared in a casual or dramatic way.

Example: "What happened at the party last night? Spill the tea!"

Cultural Note: Gen Z's love for storytelling and drama makes "Tea" a key part of their conversational repertoire.

TFW (That Feeling When)

Definition: Used to preface a relatable or emotional moment, often accompanied by a meme or image.
Example: "TFW you realize it's Monday tomorrow."
Cultural Note: Perfectly encapsulates Gen Z's use of humor and relatability in digital communication.

Toxic

Definition: Describes something harmful, manipulative, or unhealthy, whether it's a person, relationship, or environment.
Example: "That friend group is so toxic."
Cultural Note: Gen Z uses "Toxic" to call out negativity while advocating for mental health and boundaries.

Try-Hard

Definition: Someone who puts in excessive effort to impress or fit in, often to the point of seeming insincere.

Example: "He's always name-dropping celebrities—total try-hard vibes."

Cultural Note: Gen Z values authenticity and uses "Try-Hard" as a playful critique of over-the-top behavior.

Trendy

Definition: Something currently popular, stylish, or relevant.

Example: "Those cargo pants are so trendy right now."

Cultural Note: Gen Z loves embracing and remixing trends, often with a touch of irony.

Touch Grass

Definition: A humorous way to tell someone to take a break from the internet and reconnect with reality.

Example: "You've been gaming for 10 hours straight—go touch grass."

Cultural Note: Reflects Gen Z's awareness of digital burnout and the need for balance.

Take the L

Definition: To accept a loss, failure, or mistake with humility or humor.
Example: "I tripped in front of everyone—had to take the L on that one."
Cultural Note: Gen Z's use of "Take the L" shows their resilience and ability to laugh at themselves.

Typing...

Definition: Used to describe suspense or anticipation when someone is taking a long time to reply, often in a playful or sarcastic way.
Example: "He's been 'typing...' for five minutes now—just send the text!"
Cultural Note: A lighthearted way to comment on digital communication habits.

U

Unbothered, UwU, and the Unapologetic Vernacular of Gen Z

The letter "U" in Gen Z's dictionary is all about embracing calm confidence, quirky expressions, and lighthearted vibes. From staying "Unbothered" by drama to expressing cuteness with "UwU," "U" captures the unique, unapologetic energy of Gen Z's communication style. Let's uncover the unforgettable language of "U."

Unbothered

Definition: Completely unfazed, calm, or unaffected by negativity or drama.
Example: "She didn't even react to the gossip—so unbothered."
Cultural Note: Gen Z uses "Unbothered" as a badge of confidence and maturity in the face of chaos.

UwU

Definition: A text-based emoticon representing cuteness or affection, often used ironically or sincerely.
Example: "Your cat is so fluffy, UwU!"
Cultural Note: Borrowed from anime and gaming culture, "UwU" reflects Gen Z's playful embrace of internet trends.

Ult

Definition: Short for "ultimate bias" in K-pop fandoms; refers to someone's favorite artist or group.
Example: "Jimin is my ult, no question."
Cultural Note: Reflecting Gen Z's passion for fandoms, "Ult" is a term of deep admiration and loyalty.

Upcycle

Definition: Transforming old or discarded items into something new and useful, often with a creative touch.
Example: "She upcycled her old jeans into a cute tote bag."
Cultural Note: Gen Z's focus on sustainability makes "Upcycle" a key term in their eco-conscious mindset.

Unfollow

Definition: To stop following someone on social media, often signaling disinterest or disagreement.
Example: "His posts were so annoying, so I had to unfollow."
Cultural Note: For Gen Z, "Unfollow" is both a digital boundary and a subtle social statement.

Understood the Assignment

Definition: A phrase used to praise someone who excels or perfectly executes a task or look.
Example: "Her Halloween costume? She understood the assignment!"
Cultural Note: Gen Z uses this term to celebrate success and creativity with flair.

Ugh

Definition: An exclamation expressing frustration, annoyance, or exhaustion.

Example: "Ugh, I can't believe it's Monday already."
Cultural Note: Simple yet expressive, "Ugh" is a versatile way for Gen Z to vent in a relatable way.

Unreal

Definition: Used to describe something amazing, unbelievable, or exceptionally good.
Example: "Her performance was unreal."
Cultural Note: Highlights Gen Z's flair for dramatic positivity in describing standout moments.

Unalive

Definition: A euphemism for death or dying, often used humorously or to avoid triggering language.
Example: "My phone battery is unalive."
Cultural Note: Reflecting Gen Z's blend of sensitivity and humor, "Unalive" shows their creativity with language.

Upgrade

Definition: To improve or enhance something, often referring to lifestyle, relationships, or technology.

Example: "She upgraded her laptop and it's so fast now."

Cultural Note: Gen Z's focus on self-improvement and staying current makes "Upgrade" a natural part of their vernacular.

V

Vibe Check, Valid, and the Vibrant Vocabulary of Gen Z

The letter "V" in Gen Z's dictionary is all about vibes, authenticity, and versatility. From passing the "Vibe Check" to being "Valid," these terms highlight the generation's focus on energy, acceptance, and creative expression. Let's venture into the vivacious world of "V."

Vibe Check

Definition: A quick assessment of someone's energy, mood, or overall vibe, often used humorously or as a form of validation.

Example: "He showed up with donuts—he definitely passed the vibe check."

Cultural Note: Gen Z's use of "Vibe Check" reflects their emphasis on energy and alignment in social situations.

Valid

Definition: Something or someone that is genuine, cool, or deserving of respect.
Example: "That opinion is valid, and I support it."
Cultural Note: Gen Z's use of "Valid" is a nod to their appreciation for authenticity and self-expression.

Viral

Definition: Describes content that spreads rapidly across the internet, gaining widespread attention and engagement.
Example: "Her TikTok went viral overnight."
Cultural Note: Gen Z thrives on the power of virality, recognizing it as a modern marker of influence and relevance.

Vibes

Definition: The atmosphere, mood, or feeling of a person, place, or situation.
Example: "This coffee shop has such chill vibes."

Cultural Note: Vibes are central to Gen Z's language, reflecting their focus on emotional resonance and aesthetics.

Villain Era

Definition: A playful term for a phase in someone's life where they prioritize themselves, often unapologetically.
Example: "She's saying no to everyone and living her best life—total villain era."
Cultural Note: Reflects Gen Z's embrace of self-care and boundaries, even if it means being a little selfish.

Verified

Definition: Officially recognized, often referring to the blue checkmark on social media platforms signifying authenticity.
Example: "He's verified on Instagram now—big moves!"
Cultural Note: Being "Verified" is a symbol of status and legitimacy in the digital age.

Vanity Metrics

Definition: Surface-level statistics, like likes and followers, that may not reflect true success or value.
Example: "Don't focus on vanity metrics—it's about genuine engagement."
Cultural Note: Gen Z's nuanced understanding of social media highlights their ability to distinguish real impact from superficial numbers.

Vaxxed and Waxed

Definition: A humorous phrase describing someone who is vaccinated and ready to go out and enjoy life.
Example: "Summer 2021 was all about being vaxxed and waxed."
Cultural Note: Reflects Gen Z's ability to mix humor with cultural moments and trends.

Verified Vibes Only

Definition: A playful way of saying that only authentic, good energy is allowed.

Example: "This weekend is for verified vibes only."
Cultural Note: Gen Z's focus on curating positive experiences shines through this phrase.

W

Wildin', W, and the Whimsical World of Gen Z

The letter "W" in Gen Z's dictionary is filled with wins, wit, and whimsical expressions. From celebrating victories ("W") to embracing chaotic fun ("Wildin'"), this chapter dives into the wonderful ways Gen Z uses language to connect and entertain. Let's explore the winning vocabulary of "W."

W

Definition: Short for "win," used to signify success, positivity, or something desirable.
Example: "Scored tickets to the concert—big W!"
Cultural Note: Gen Z uses "W" to celebrate achievements, no matter how big or small.

Wildin'

Definition: Acting out of control, being overly dramatic, or engaging in chaotic behavior.
Example: "He was wildin' at the party last night!"
Cultural Note: A playful way to describe someone's over-the-top actions, often with a mix of humor and exasperation.

We Move

Definition: A phrase used to express resilience, moving on, or adapting to challenges.
Example: "Missed the bus this morning, but we move."
Cultural Note: Reflects Gen Z's ability to maintain a positive outlook in the face of setbacks.

Wholesome

Definition: Something pure, uplifting, or heartwarming.
Example: "That video of the grandma dancing was so wholesome."
Cultural Note: Gen Z cherishes wholesome content as a break from the chaos of everyday life.

Woke

Definition: A term originally signifying awareness of social issues, now often used sarcastically to critique performative activism.
Example: "He posted one infographic and now he thinks he's woke."
Cultural Note: While "woke" has serious origins, Gen Z often uses it to balance sincerity and satire in discussions about social justice.

Win-Win

Definition: A situation where everyone benefits or comes out ahead.
Example: "Splitting the prize money was a win-win for both of us."
Cultural Note: Highlights Gen Z's appreciation for fairness and collaboration.

Way Too Much

Definition: Used to describe something excessive, overwhelming, or extra.

Example: "The drama in this group chat is way too much."

Cultural Note: Gen Z's humor thrives on exaggeration, making this phrase a staple for playful complaints.

What's the Move?

Definition: A phrase used to ask about plans or the next step in a situation.

Example: "It's Friday night—what's the move?"

Cultural Note: Reflects Gen Z's spontaneous and social approach to decision-making.

Wild

Definition: Describes something crazy, unbelievable, or unexpected.

Example: "That plot twist in the movie was wild."

Cultural Note: A versatile term, "Wild" is often used to express amazement or disbelief.

Winning

Definition: A phrase used to describe someone who is succeeding or thriving in life.

Example: "You just got a promotion and a new car? You're winning!"

Cultural Note: Reflects Gen Z's enthusiasm for celebrating successes, big or small.

X

XOXO, Extra, and the X-factor of Gen Z Language

The letter "X" in Gen Z's dictionary may be sparse, but it's filled with expressions that are playful, versatile, and impactful. From virtual hugs and kisses ("XOXO") to being a little "eXtra," "X" showcases how this generation redefines and repurposes language in creative ways. Let's examine the expressive entries of "X."

XOXO

Definition: A sign-off or message of affection, symbolizing hugs and kisses.
Example: "Thanks for the advice! XOXO."
Cultural Note: While classic in origin, "XOXO" remains a lighthearted and affectionate way for Gen Z to end texts, often with a hint of irony.

Extra (The X in Extra)

Definition: Over-the-top, dramatic, or doing more than necessary.

Example: "She brought a full cake to the picnic—so extra!"

Cultural Note: Though not strictly starting with "X," "Extra" captures Gen Z's flair for calling out extravagant behavior in a fun and endearing way.

X Games Mode

Definition: A phrase used to describe someone doing something extreme, impressive, or unexpected.

Example: "He just jumped over the fence like he was in X Games mode!"

Cultural Note: Inspired by extreme sports, this term is often used humorously to highlight moments of unexpected skill or boldness.

Xennial

Definition: Refers to individuals born on the cusp of Gen X and Millennials, often used to poke fun at generational overlaps.

Example: "My older sister is a Xennial and doesn't get

TikTok humor."

Cultural Note: While Gen Z embraces generational labels, they often use them playfully to describe shared but distinct experiences.

X Marks the Spot

Definition: A phrase signaling the discovery of something important, valuable, or noteworthy.

Example: "Found the perfect outfit—X marks the spot!"

Cultural Note: Gen Z loves reinventing classic phrases for contemporary use, blending nostalgia with modern context.

Y

Yeet, Yass Queen, and the Youthful Yell of Gen Z

The letter "Y" in Gen Z's dictionary is filled with energy, empowerment, and enthusiasm. From expressive exclamations ("Yeet") to celebratory affirmations ("Yass Queen"), "Y" reflects the generation's zest for life and language. Let's dive into the youthful and dynamic entries of "Y."

Yeet

Definition: An exclamation used to express excitement, or as a verb, to throw something with force or abandon.
Example: "He yeeted his backpack across the room."
Cultural Note: Yeet is versatile, representing Gen Z's humor and spontaneity, often used in memes and viral content.

Yass Queen

Definition: A phrase used to celebrate and hype someone up, often in response to their confidence, style, or accomplishments.

Example: "She absolutely slayed her performance—yass queen!"

Cultural Note: Rooted in LGBTQ+ culture, this expression is now widely used to show support and admiration.

YOLO (You Only Live Once)

Definition: A phrase encouraging boldness and living in the moment.

Example: "I bought the concert tickets—YOLO!"

Cultural Note: While it gained traction in earlier generations, YOLO remains relevant in Gen Z's vocabulary as a reminder to seize opportunities.

You're Built Different

Definition: A phrase used to compliment someone's unique qualities, strength, or abilities.

Example: "He ran a marathon without training—he's

built different."
Cultural Note: This term reflects Gen Z's creative way of acknowledging individuality and excellence.

You're Him/Her

Definition: A phrase used to praise someone as exceptional, often implying they are the best at what they do.
Example: "After that game-winning shot, you're him!"
Cultural Note: Gen Z uses this phrase to elevate others with a mix of admiration and confidence.

You Good?

Definition: A casual way of checking in on someone's well-being or asking if everything is okay.
Example: "You've been quiet all day—you good?"
Cultural Note: Highlights Gen Z's emphasis on emotional awareness and casual care.

Your Vibes Are Immaculate

Definition: A phrase used to compliment someone's positive energy, presence, or overall mood.

Example: "She's so fun to be around—her vibes are immaculate."

Cultural Note: Reflects Gen Z's focus on energy and connection in relationships.

Z

Zoomer, Zaddy, and the Zesty Zingers of Gen Z

The letter "Z" in Gen Z's dictionary represents boldness, charm, and generational pride. From generational nicknames ("Zoomer") to playful compliments ("Zaddy"), this chapter dives into the vibrant and cheeky expressions that make "Z" stand out. Let's zigzag through the zesty language of "Z."

Zoomer

Definition: A nickname for members of Generation Z, often used humorously or affectionately.
Example: "As a proud Zoomer, I love TikTok trends."
Cultural Note: While "Boomer" inspired the term, "Zoomer" reflects Gen Z's tech-savvy, fast-paced culture.

Zaddy

Definition: A term for an attractive, stylish, and confident man, often implying maturity and charisma.
Example: "That actor in the new movie? Total zaddy."
Cultural Note: Gen Z uses "Zaddy" as a playful yet admiring compliment, blending humor with genuine appreciation.

Zoned Out

Definition: To lose focus or drift into a daydream-like state, often unintentionally.
Example: "I totally zoned out during that lecture."
Cultural Note: A universal experience, "Zoned Out" is Gen Z's way of describing their moments of mental escape.

Zero Chill

Definition: Acting overly dramatic, excitable, or lacking composure.
Example: "He yelled at the ref—zero chill."
Cultural Note: A humorous way to critique exaggerated reactions, "Zero Chill" showcases Gen Z's playful approach to calling out behavior.

Zen

Definition: A state of calm, peace, or mindfulness.
Example: "Meditation helps me stay in my zen."
Cultural Note: Reflects Gen Z's interest in mental health and self-care practices.

Zombied

Definition: A new twist on ghosting, where someone suddenly reappears in your life after previously cutting off contact.
Example: "He didn't text me for months, and now he's zombied me out of nowhere."
Cultural Note: Gen Z's clever updates to dating lingo keep their language fresh and relevant.

Zero Waste

Definition: A lifestyle aimed at reducing waste and environmental impact.
Example: "She's all about that zero-waste life."

Cultural Note: Highlights Gen Z's focus on sustainability and eco-conscious living.

Zigged When You Should Have Zagged

Definition: A phrase describing a misstep or wrong decision, often used humorously.
Example: "I tried to freestyle that recipe and zigged when I should have zagged."
Cultural Note: Reflects Gen Z's love for quirky phrases that turn mistakes into lighthearted moments.

Fun Extras

What's Your Gen Z Lingo Fluency?

Ready to put your Gen Z lingo skills to the test? Below is a fun quiz designed to see if you can vibe with the language of the Zoomer generation. Whether you're a slang expert or just learning the ropes, this is your chance to flex your knowledge and have a laugh along the way.

Part 1: Fill in the Blank

1. When someone is really attractive, you might call them a ___________. (Hint: It's a snack, but not for eating!)
2. If someone says, "No cap," they're telling you the ___________.
3. "That movie was so mid," means it was ___________.
4. If you hear "Yass Queen!" it's probably being said to ___________ someone.
5. A ___________ check is all about seeing if someone's energy or attitude matches the vibe.

6. When someone says they were "ghosted," it means someone _____________ them.
7. To "spill the tea" means to share _____________.
8. A "simp" is someone who tries too hard to _____________ someone they like.
9. Saying "It's giving..." is a way to _____________ something's vibe.
10. To "Stan" someone means to be a _____________ fan of them.
11. If someone tells you to "touch grass," they mean you should _____________.
12. A "savage" comment is one that is _____________.
13. "Receipts" refer to _____________ that back up your claim.
14. "Hard launch" is the _____________ reveal of something new, like a relationship.
15. "Sus" is short for _____________.
16. A "soft launch" is a _____________ way of introducing something new.
17. If someone is being "extra," they are _____________.
18. "Built different" means someone is _____________ or unique.
19. A "squad" refers to your _____________ group.
20. "Viral" describes something that is _____________ shared online.
21. If someone "takes an L," they _____________ at something.

22. Saying "savage" about someone means they were
__________ bold.
23. "Mood" is a term that describes something
__________ relatable.
24. A "hard flex" is when someone shows off in a
__________ way.
25. To "slay" means to __________ at something.

Part 2: Multiple Choice

1. What does "Extra" mean?
   - a) Over-the-top
   - b) Average
   - c) Simple
   - d) Calm

2. If someone says "That's cap," they mean:
   - a) It's true
   - b) It's a lie
   - c) It's amazing
   - d) It's confusing

3. What does "Built Different" mean?
   - a) Someone is unique or exceptional
   - b) Someone is physically strong
   - c) Someone is overly emotional
   - d) Someone is out of shape

4. "Vibe Check" is about:
   - a) Testing someone's mood or energy

- o   b) Asking for a new playlist
- o   c) Requesting money
- o   d) Planning an event
5.   What does "Simp" mean?
- o   a) A confident leader
- o   b) A fan of anime
- o   c) Someone overly eager to please
- o   d) A style icon
6.   "No Chill" describes someone who is:
- o   a) Calm
- o   b) Overly dramatic
- o   c) Silent
- o   d) Joyful
7.   What does "Ghosting" mean?
- o   a) Ignoring someone suddenly
- o   b) Dressing as a ghost
- o   c) Talking non-stop
- o   d) Sending gifts anonymously
8.   What does "Mood" mean?
- o   a) A general feeling or vibe
- o   b) An awkward situation
- o   c) A complicated problem
- o   d) A strict rule
9.   "Hard Launch" refers to:
- o   a) A big announcement
- o   b) A new workout move
- o   c) A failed attempt
- o   d) A party theme

10. What does "Receipts" mean?

- a) Evidence
- b) Coupons
- c) Drama
- d) Invitations

11. What does "Savage" mean?

- a) Bold or fearless
- b) Calm and collected
- c) Shy and reserved
- d) Confused

12. What does "Soft Launch" refer to?

- a) A subtle introduction
- b) A tough decision
- c) A slow-moving vehicle
- d) A loud argument

13. "Yeet" can be used to mean:

- a) Throw something forcefully
- b) Greet someone politely
- c) Dance quietly
- d) Cry dramatically

14. What does "Slay" mean?

- a) To excel or impress
- b) To criticize someone
- c) To make a mistake
- d) To leave abruptly

15. "Valid" means:

- a) Cool or respectable
- b) Uncertain

- c) Aggressive
- d) Outdated

16. "Touch Grass" means:

- a) Go outside and disconnect
- b) Learn to garden
- c) Start a conversation
- d) Relax indoors

17. "Yass Queen" is often used to:

- a) Encourage someone
- b) Criticize someone
- c) Describe food
- d) Express confusion

18. "Take the L" means:

- a) Accept a loss
- b) Celebrate success
- c) Go on a trip
- d) Give advice

19. "Savage" can describe:

- a) A bold or fearless action
- b) A quiet retreat
- c) A peaceful moment
- d) A silly mistake

20. What does "Simp" imply?

- a) Overly invested in someone
- b) Ignoring a relationship
- c) Playing video games
- d) Being extremely brave

21. "Mood" is:

- a) Relatable energy
- b) Awkward silence
- c) Emotional regret
- d) A strict rule

22. A "Stan" is:
- a) A devoted fan
- b) A harsh critic
- c) A quiet observer
- d) A random stranger

23. "Receipts" most often mean:
- a) Proof
- b) Money
- c) Drama
- d) Relationships

24. "No Chill" describes someone who:
- a) Overreacts dramatically
- b) Stays calm in chaos
- c) Loves cold weather
- d) Avoids conflict

25. "Zero Chill" can also be described as:
- a) Lacking composure
- b) Feeling peaceful
- c) Taking a step back
- d) Enjoying a win

Part 3: True or False

1. "Built Different" is a compliment. (True/False)
2. "Mood" is used to describe something relatable. (True/False)
3. "Receipts" are actual paper receipts from stores. (True/False)
4. Saying "No Cap" means you're being honest. (True/False)
5. "Ghosting" means suddenly cutting off contact with someone. (True/False)
6. "Hard Launch" is about subtly revealing something. (True/False)
7. "Savage" is a term used to describe someone being shy. (True/False)
8. "Simp" is a term for someone who shows excessive admiration. (True/False)
9. "Vibe Check" is about testing someone's mood. (True/False)
10. "Slay" means to fail at something. (True/False)
11. "Soft Launch" is a quiet way to introduce something new. (True/False)
12. "Yeet" can be used to express excitement. (True/False)
13. "Extra" means someone is doing too much. (True/False)
14. "Touch Grass" means to take a break from the internet. (True/False)

15. "Zero Chill" means someone is acting overly dramatic. (True/False)
16. "Mood" is a term for strict rules. (True/False)
17. "Take the L" means to accept a win. (True/False)
18. "Stan" is used for devoted fans. (True/False)
19. "Yass Queen" criticizes people. (True/False)
20. "Receipts" refer to proof. (True/False)
21. "Simp" describes someone detached. (True/False)
22. "Viral" relates to broad online sharing. (True/False)
23. "Extra" means being understated. (True/False)
24. "Mood" is unrelated to relatability. (True/False)
25. "Slay" is about excelling. (True/False)

Scoring

- **55-75 Points**: You're fluent! You're basically a Gen Z dictionary yourself.
- **40-54 Points**: You've got solid knowledge, but there's room to level up.
- **25-39 Points**: Not bad! You're picking up the vibes, but keep studying.
- **0-24 Points**: Time to dive back into the dictionary—there's a whole world of slang to explore!

Answers:

Part 1: Fill in the Blank

1. Snack
2. Truth
3. Mediocre
4. Hype
5. Vibe
6. Ignored
7. Gossip
8. Impress
9. Describe
10. Devoted
11. Go outside
12. Bold
13. Proof
14. Official
15. Suspicious
16. Subtle
17. Over-the-top
18. Exceptional
19. Friend
20. Widely
21. Fail
22. Boldly
23. Relatable
24. Showy
25. Excel

Part 2: Multiple Choice

1. a) Over-the-top
2. b) It's a lie
3. a) Someone is unique or exceptional
4. a) Testing someone's mood or energy

5. c) Someone overly eager to please
6. b) Overly dramatic
7. a) Ignoring someone suddenly
8. a) A general feeling or vibe
9. a) A big announcement
10. a) Evidence
11. a) Bold or fearless
12. a) A subtle introduction
13. a) Throw something forcefully
14. a) To excel or impress
15. a) Cool or respectable
16. a) Go outside and disconnect
17. a) Encourage someone
18. a) Accept a loss
19. a) A bold or fearless action
20. a) Overly invested in someone
21. a) Relatable energy
22. a) A devoted fan
23. a) Proof
24. a) Overreacts dramatically
25. a) Lacking composure

Part 3: True or False

1. True   2. True   3. False

4. True	11. True	18. True
5. True	12. True	19. False
6. False	13. True	20. True
7. False	14. True	21. False
8. True	15. True	22. True
9. True	16. False	23. False
10. False	17. False	24. False
		25. True